The Frog in the Pond

UNSWORTH ELEMENTARY
5685 UNSWORTH RD.
CHILLIWACK B.C. V2R 4P5

by **Dana Meachen Rau**

Reading Consultant: Nanci R. Vargus, Ed. D.

Marshall Cavendish
Benchmark
New York

Picture Words

 balloon

 cattails

 dragonfly

 ducks

 feet

 fish

frog

 frog's

 legs

 lily pad

 pond

 snake

 sun

A  lives in the .

The  rests on a .

4

The  keeps the

warm.

The looks for food.

6

Here comes a .

The shoots out its tongue. Yum!

A 🐍 in the 🌾 is hungry, too.

The 🐍 is looking for a 🐸 to eat.

The  sees the .

The  leaps into the
.

The 🐸's back 🦵
help it jump.

Now the 🐸 is safe.

The 's help
it swim.

The swims with
and .

The climbs onto a again.

18

The 🐸 sings.

The 🐸's throat blows up like a 🎈.

Words to Know

hungry (HUHNG-ree)
    to want food

leaps (leeps)
    jumps

shoots moves very fast

throat (throht)
    the area under the chin

Find Out More

Books

Arnosky, Jim. *All About Frogs*. New York: Scholastic, 2002.

French, Vivian. *Growing Frogs*. Cambridge, MA: Candlewick Press, 2000.

Kalman, Bobbie and Jacqueline Langille. *What Is An Amphibian?* New York: Crabtree Publishing Company, 2000.

Videos

Magic School Bus Hops Home, KidVision.

See How They Grow: Pond Animals, Sony Wonder.

Web Sites

Exploratorium: Frogs
http://www.exploratorium.edu/frogs/index.html

Frogland!
http://allaboutfrogs.org/froglnd.shtml

Smithsonian National Zoological Park
http://nationalzoo.si.edu

About the Author

Dana Meachen Rau is an author, editor, and illustrator. A graduate of Trinity College in Hartford, Connecticut, she has written more than one hundred books for children, including nonfiction, biographies, early readers, and historical fiction. She finds frogs in her backyard garden in Burlington, Connecticut, especially after it rains.

About the Reading Consultant

Nanci R. Vargus, Ed.D, wants all children to enjoy reading. She used to teach first grade. Now she works at the University of Indianapolis. Nanci helps young people become teachers. When her daughters were little, they would watch the frogs that lived beside the backyard creek.

Marshall Cavendish Benchmark
99 White Plains Road
Tarrytown, NY 10591-9001
www.marshallcavendish.us

All Internet sites were correct at the time of printing.

Library of Congress Cataloging-In-Data

Rau, Dana Meachen, 1971–
The frog in the pond / by Dana Meachen Rau
        p. cm. — (Benchmark rebus)
Summary: "A rebus book about a frog and his home in the pond"—Provided by publisher.
Includes bibliographical references.
ISBN-13: 978-0-7614-2310-2
ISBN-10: 0-7614-2310-9
Frogs—Juvenile literature. I. Title. II. Series.
QL668.E2R38 2006
597.8—dc22
        2005029051

Editor: Christine Florie
Editorial Director: Michelle Bisson
Art Director: Anahid Hamparian
Series Designer: Virginia Pope

Photo research by Connie Gardner

Rebus images provided courtesy of *Dorling Kindersley.*

Cover photo by Jim Battles/*Dembinsky Photo Associates*

The photographs in this book are used with permission and through the courtesy of:
Corbis: p. 5 Roger Tidman; p. 13 Joe McDonald; p. 17 Gary W. Carter; p. 21 Joe McDonald; Getty: p. 7 Stone;
Dembinsky Photo Associates: p. 9 Gary Meszaros; p. 19 Jim Battles; *Photo Researchers*: p. 11 Steve and Dave Maslowski;
DRK Photo: p. 15 Joe McDonald

Printed in Malaysia
1 3 5 6 4 2